TECHNICAL REPORT

Early Results on Activations and the Earnings of Reservists

Jacob Alex Klerman, David S. Loughran, Craig Martin

Prepared for the Office of the Secretary of Defense

T0159303

RAND NATIONAL DEFENSE RESEARCH INSTITUTE

The research described in this report was prepared for the Office of the Secretary of Defense (OSD). The research was conducted in the RAND National Defense Research Institute, a federally funded research and development center supported by the OSD, the Joint Staff, the unified commands, and the defense agencies under Contract DASW01-01-C-0004.

Library of Congress Cataloging-in-Publication Data

Klerman, Jacob Alex.
    Early results on activations and the earnings of reservists / Jacob Alex Klerman, David S. Loughran, Craig Martin.
      p. cm.
    "TR-274."
    Includes bibliographical references.
    ISBN 0-8330-3819-2 (pbk. : alk. paper)
    1. United States—Armed Forces—Reserves—Pay, allowances, etc.—Statistics. 2. United States—Armed Forces—Mobilization—Costs—Statistics. 3. Wage surveys—United States. I. Loughran, David S., 1969– II. Martin, Craig, 1968– III.Title.

UA42.K635 2005
355.3'7'0973—dc22

2005016178

The RAND Corporation is a nonprofit research organization providing objective analysis and effective solutions that address the challenges facing the public and private sectors around the world. RAND's publications do not necessarily reflect the opinions of its research clients and sponsors.

RAND® is a registered trademark.

Published 2005 by the RAND Corporation
1776 Main Street, P.O. Box 2138, Santa Monica, CA 90407-2138
1200 South Hayes Street, Arlington, VA 22202-5050
201 North Craig Street, Suite 202, Pittsburgh, PA 15213-1516
RAND URL: http://www.rand.org/
To order RAND documents or to obtain additional information, contact
Distribution Services: Telephone: (310) 451-7002;
Fax: (310) 451-6915; Email: order@rand.org

PREFACE

This document reports early estimates of how activations in support of the Global War on Terrorism affect the earnings of reservists. The document was produced as part of the RAND project "The Effect of Activation on the Earnings of Reservists." That project matches administrative data on activations and military compensation from the Department of Defense (DoD) to data on civilian earnings from the Social Security Administration (SSA) to estimate the effect of activation on the earnings of reservists while they are serving on active duty. Understanding the short-term effect of activation on the earnings of reservists is crucial for designing an efficient and equitable compensation system for the reserve components.

This document provides analyses based on 2001 civilian earnings recorded by SSA for a sample of reservists activated for the Global War on Terrorism in 2001 and 2002. It uses this information to project civilian earnings for 2001. It then uses administrative data on military pay recorded by the Defense Manpower Data Center for Army and Air Force reservists to project monthly military earnings in 2002 and 2003.

The sample of reservists on which this report relies is not ideal and constrains our methodological approach in a number of important ways. A final document will employ a more comprehensive sample of reservists and report results from a more complete set of analyses. Those follow-on analyses will employ data on civilian earnings for all reservists for 2000 through 2003 and military earnings through 2004. This expanded database will allow us to consider Navy and Marine reservists, incorporate better controls for observed and unobserved heterogeneity, analyze a larger sample, and provide more disaggregated estimates of earnings impacts attributable to activation.

This research was conducted for the Office of the Secretary of Defense-Reserve Affairs within the Forces and Resources Policy Center of the RAND National Defense Research Institute (NDRI). NDRI, a division of the RAND Corporation, is a federally funded research and development center sponsored by the Office of the Secretary of Defense, the Joint Staff, the unified commands, and the defense agencies.

For more information on RAND's Forces and Resources Policy Center, contact the Acting Director, James Hosek. He can be reached by email at

James_Hosek@rand.org; by phone at 310-393-0411, extension 7183; or by mail at the RAND Corporation, 1776 Main Street, Santa Monica, California 90407-2138. More information about RAND is available at http://www.rand.org.

CONTENTS

TABLES

SUMMARY

INTRODUCTION

In conducting the Global War on Terrorism, the Department of Defense (DoD) has relied heavily on the reserve components. A large fraction of the reserve force has been activated at least once since September 11, 2001, and many of these activations have lasted for more than a year. This more intensive use of the Reserves has been accompanied by concerns that many reservists suffer substantial financial losses as a result of being activated. A number of legislative proposals at the federal and state levels would increase compensation of activated reservists to offset these financial losses.[1]

This report describes research using a sample of Army and Air Force reservists activated in 2001 and 2002 for the Global War on Terrorism. For those reservists, we combine information on civilian earnings from Social Security Administration (SSA) data for 2001 with information on military earnings from DoD administrative files to construct an estimate of the effect of activation on the earnings of reservists. Our measure of military earnings includes pays, allowances, and an approximation to the value of the federal tax preference accorded military allowances and military pay received while serving in a combat zone. Specifically, we use SSA data for calendar year 2001 to extrapolate full-year civilian earnings of reservists who served on active duty in 2002 and 2003. Because we only have data on civilian earnings in 2001, we cannot reliably compute total earnings in 2002 and 2003. Instead, we use military pay data for reservists who served on active duty during 2002 and 2003 to extrapolate full-year military earnings for those reservists. For each activated reservist, we then compute the difference between annualized military earnings while serving on active duty in 2002 and 2003 and annualized civilian earnings derived from the 2001 SSA data. We then compute the average difference and the fraction of activated reservists experiencing any earnings

---

[1] We use the term "activated" throughout this document to refer generically to a state of serving on active duty, whether it be active duty for training or serving on active duty voluntarily or involuntarily as part of a mobilization or other call to active duty.

loss or an earnings loss of at least $10,000 or 10 percent of earnings when not activated.

ESTIMATED DIFFERENCE IN EARNINGS

Contrary to stories in the popular press and analyses of self-reported earning loss data recorded in DoD surveys, our analyses of administrative data indicate that most (72 percent) reservists experience a significant increase in earnings. The average increase in earnings of activated reservists is over $850 per month (in 2003 dollars), which represents an increase of 25 percent over earnings when they were not activated; 65 percent of reservists in our sample experience earnings increases of more than 10 percent. However, a sizable fraction of activated reservists (28 percent) experience some loss in earnings and for some (20 percent) of these reservists, the losses represent 10 percent or more of their earnings when not activated. For those with long activations in later years (more than 270 days in 2002 or 2003), but short or no activation(s) in the base year (90 days or less in 2001), average earnings gains are larger (more than $1,500 per month or 44 percent of earnings when not activated), the fraction experiencing any earnings loss is smaller (17 percent experience any loss), and the fraction with severe earnings losses is also smaller (11 percent experience a loss of 10 percent or more).

Our estimates of earnings losses are smaller for those serving on active duty in 2003 compared to those serving on active duty in 2002. Overall, 32 percent of the reservists in our sample activated in 2002 experienced some earnings loss compared to 23 percent of reservists activated in 2003. We estimate smaller earnings losses in 2003 than in 2002 across a range of activation patterns and measures of earnings gains and losses. The difference in estimated earnings changes in 2003 and 2002 is due primarily to higher military pay in 2003 than in 2002 due to pay increases, increased receipt of special pays, promotions within our sample, and changes in the composition of activated reservists.

Our estimates of earnings changes are also sensitive to the number of days served on active duty. Those reservists serving for longer periods on active duty are less likely to experience earnings losses than those reservists serving for shorter periods on active duty. This difference appears to be because reservists serving for long periods on active duty have higher full-year equivalent military earnings because they are more likely to receive family separation allowance, hostile fire pay, and the combat zone tax exclusion. In addition, these reservists have lower civilian pay. One reason reservists with long periods of active duty service have lower civilian pay could be that those with lower civilian pay are more likely to volunteer for activation and longer periods of active duty.

Compared to those serving more than 270 days on active duty in a calendar year, those serving 270 days or less on active duty in a calendar year experience smaller average earnings gains and a larger fraction of these reservists experience some earnings loss. Earnings gains are smallest and the prevalence of earnings losses largest among reservists serving 90 days or less on active duty in a calendar year. For that group of reservists, 38 percent experience an earnings loss, and 29 percent experience one of 10 percent or more.

DISCUSSION

The results on earnings and activation reported in this document are early and subject to a number of important caveats. First, these results are based on a pre-existing sample of reservists activated in 2001 and 2002 for the Global War on Terrorism. We are currently working to expand our sample to include all reservists activated following September 11, 2001. Second, our sample excludes reservists serving in the Navy and Marine Corps. Third, the approach taken here compares earnings prior to activation to earnings received when activated. Our analysis does not consider what would have happened to the earnings of reservists had they not been activated. Fourth, our estimates do not consider several sources of compensation received when serving on active duty. These include employer "top-off" and the expected present discounted value of accumulated retirement points.

Finally, these estimates refer to an important, but narrowly defined outcome: earnings. We thus ignore any increase in household costs, any business losses, any effects on spousal earnings, and any non-financial costs (or benefits) attributable to activation and deployment. Thus, standard compensation arguments imply that, inasmuch as the reserve components are experiencing recruiting and retention problems, the conventional incentive case for raising reserve compensation remains valid.

Our estimates imply less prevalent and severe earnings losses among activated reservists than do estimates derived from DoD survey data. The reason for this difference in estimates is likely related to both sampling and measurement issues. Our sample is composed of Army and Air Force reservists activated in either 2001 or 2002 in support of the Global War on Terrorism. DoD survey estimates are based on a sample of reservists responding to their survey (and the earnings loss questions), which may or may not be representative of all reservists. Our estimates are derived from administrative data on earnings which we believe are well defined, highly accurate, and comprehensive. DoD survey estimates are based on self-reported estimates of civilian and military income and those estimates may be inaccurate. Perhaps most significantly, DoD survey questions do not solicit estimates of the value of the tax advantage accorded some military earnings when serving on active duty, a component of pay that we find to be important.

Prior to September 11, 2001, most reservists reasonably thought that the likelihood of being involuntary activated for a lengthy period of time was low. Thus, even individuals who were at risk of suffering significant earnings losses when activated might nonetheless enlist or reenlist in the Reserves. However, it is likely that DoD's intensive use of the Reserves since September 11, 2001, has caused existing and potential reservists to revise their expectations regarding the likelihood of activation upward. Consequently, all else equal, we expect that fewer individuals with large potential earnings losses will enlist or reenlist in the Reserves in the future, which should result in even smaller aggregate earnings losses than we report here.

There are pros and cons associated with the departure from the Reserves of reservists with large potential earnings losses. On the one hand, perhaps reservists who stand to suffer large losses, like the self-employed or individuals who command large civilian salaries, are not a good match in aggregate for a Reserve force that DoD wishes to use with some frequency. On the other hand, many of these individuals could possess skills that are particularly valued by the Reserves, making their departure problematic for maintaining desired capabilities and readiness in the Reserves. How to compensate individuals with large earnings losses whom DoD wishes to retain is unclear and should be the focus of future research.

Regardless of what policies DoD enacts to address earnings loss in the future, we recommend that DoD consider providing reservists (and potential reservists) with more information about how their military earnings are likely to change when serving on active duty. Providing this information might help DoD avoid unwittingly recruiting and retaining reservists with the potential for large earnings losses and the attendant bad publicity that occurs because of this. Conversely, providing this information might also help the Reserves retain individuals who are unaware that their military earnings could increase significantly because of the special pays they receive and the tax preference accorded earnings received while serving in a combat zone.

IMPROVING THESE ESTIMATES

The estimates of earnings changes attributable to activation reported in this document are preliminary, but we believe useful for the ongoing policy debate. The project's final report will use better data and more sophisticated analytical methods to generate a richer and more robust characterization of the effects of activation on the earnings of reservists. We expect that some of those data and methodological improvements will increase the estimated prevalence of earnings losses, while other improvements will decrease the estimated prevalence of earnings losses. The net impact of these data and methodological improvements on the estimates reported in this document is unknown.

ACKNOWLEDGMENTS

This document could not have appeared at this time without the support and cooperation of staff in the Defense Manpower Data Center (DMDC), Social Security Administration (SSA), and the Office of the Secretary of Defense-Reserve Affairs (OSD-RA). Scott Seggerman and Barbara Balison at DMDC provided data promptly, answered questions, and facilitated the transfer of data to SSA. Mike Risha at SSA expedited the processing of the formal contract for access to the data, patiently explained what data were available and how we could use them, and produced grouped earnings statistics for us.

We greatly appreciate the support of our sponsors in OSD-RA who were actively involved in developing the analysis plan for this project and shaping this document. They include Dr. John Winkler, Capt. Michael Price, Richard Krimmer, Virginia Highland, and Tom Bush.

At RAND, we have benefited from the support and guidance of the leadership of the Forces and Resources Policy Center (FRP) in the National Defense Research Institute, Susan Everingham and Meg Harrell. We also benefited from the comments of our colleagues at RAND at an internal FRP Seminar. Particularly helpful comments were received from Jim Hosek and Susan Hosek. Beth Asch and Harry Thie provided a quick and thorough review of this document. Their input is greatly appreciated. Brian Maue and Bogdan Savych provided excellent research assistance. Paul Steinberg, Claudia McCowan, and Christopher Dirks provided excellent editorial support.

ACRONYMS

Acronym	Definition
ADT	Active Duty Training
AGR	Active Guard Reserve
BAH	Basic Allowance for Housing
BAS	Basic Allowance for Subsistence
CZTE	Combat Zone Tax Exclusion
DMDC	Defense Manpower Data Center
DoD	Department of Defense
EITC	Earned Income Tax Credit
FICA	Federal Insurance Contribution Act
FRP	Forces and Resources Policy Program
FSA	Family Separation Allowance
GWT	Global War on Terrorism
HFP	Hostile Fire Pay
IDT	Inactive Duty Training
OSD-RA	Office of the Secretary of Defense-Reserve Affairs
RMC	Regular Military Compensation (Sum of Basic Pay, Basic Allowance for Housing, Basic Allowance for Subsistence, and Tax Advantage)
RPF	Reserve Pay File
SOFRC	Status of Forces Survey of Reserve Component Members
SSA	Social Security Administration

1. INTRODUCTION

BACKGROUND

During the ongoing Global War on Terrorism (GWT), a large fraction of the reserve force has been activated and the typical activation has been involuntary and lasted a year or more. Thus, the possibility that reservists might suffer financial losses during periods of activation is a subject of considerable concern to the reserve community, policymakers, and the public.[2] Specifically, many have argued that reservists serving in harm's way should not also be subject to significant financial harm. In addition, actual and expected income losses during and after activation might discourage reservists from reenlisting and some potential reservists from enlisting at all. In an effort to address both of these concerns, there are now a number of proposals before Congress and state legislatures to increase compensation and provide other benefits for activated reservists.[3]

Both the equity and compensation perspectives on earnings losses of reservists are incorporated in the arguments for the Hope at Home Act (H.R. 838), which would require the federal government to make up the difference between civil service pay and military pay for federal employees and to offer a fifty percent tax credit (up to $30,000) for private sector employers who continue to pay reservists when serving on active duty. In a letter to colleagues dated April 12, 2005, Representative Lantos and the other cosponsors of the Hope at Home Act justified this legislation with comments reflecting an equity perspective: "Clearly the citizens who enlist in the Guard and Reserves do so because of an admirable sense of patriotism to our country. The financial security of their family should not be jeopardized because of their service to our country." Representative Lantos and colleagues also justified the legislation from a compensation perspective: "Failure to ensure the financial security for these brave men, women, and

---

[2] See, for example, the *New York Times* Editorial "Part-time Pay for Full-time Service" (March 10, 2005).

[3] We use the term "activated" throughout this document to refer generically to a state of serving on active duty, whether it be active duty for training (ADT) or serving on active duty voluntarily or involuntarily as part of a mobilization or other call to active duty.

their families is a significant roadblock to retention and recruitment for the Guard and Reserves."[4]

The concerns of policymakers and other about earnings loss are based largely on anecdotal evidence in the popular press[5] and estimates of earnings loss derived from DoD survey data. In several DoD surveys, a sizable fraction of reservists report that they suffered an income loss when activated. For example, GAO (2003) reports findings from the 2000 Reserve Component Survey in which 41 percent of responding reservists stated that their most recent activation led to a loss of earnings, 30 percent reported no change in earnings, and 29 percent reported an increase in earnings. About 10 percent of the sample reported total earnings losses of more than $5,000.

Earnings loss figures derived from the May 2004 Status of Forces Survey of Reserve Component Members (SOFRC), incorporating the experiences of reservists serving on active duty during the Global War on Terrorism, are similar. Sixty percent of the reservists surveyed in the May 2004 SOFRC report some earnings loss, 44 percent report an earnings loss of ten percent or more, and 21 percent report an earnings loss of 20 percent or more.[6]

OBJECTIVE AND ORGANIZATION OF THE DOCUMENT

This study use administrative data to estimate the change in the earnings of reservists between periods of inactive and active duty service during the Global War on Terrorism. For a sample of reservists activated for the Global War on Terrorism in 2001 and 2002, we combine information on civilian earnings from Social Security Administration (SSA) data for 2001 with information on military earnings from DoD administrative data for 2001, 2002 and 2003 to construct early estimates of the effect of full-year activation on the earnings of reservists. Follow-on analyses will use a more comprehensive sample of reservists, data on more years of civilian earnings, and more

---

[4] "Defense Department Survey Shows That Pay Gap Problem More Severe Than Initially Thought," Letter to Congress from Representative Lantos, April 12, 2005.

[5] For example, see "When Duty Calls, They Suffer", USA Today, April 17, 2003; "Reservists Under Economic Fire," USA Today, April 22, 2003; "Reservists Pay Steep Price for Service," USA Today, June 9, 2003.

[6] Authors' estimates. We restrict the SOFRC sample to reservists who are not currently serving in the Active Guard and Reserve (AGR) and who reported being activated in the past 24 months. This reduces the sample from 20,724 to 11,063 observations. Of these remaining observations, 8,217 reported earnings information such that we could compute monthly earnings before and during the respondent's most recent activation. Please refer to DMDC (2005) for more on the May 2004 SOFRC.

sophisticated analytical methods to generate improved estimates of earnings changes attributable to activation. For reasons we discuss in the body of the report and in the final chapter, our findings are not directly comparable to the previously cited DoD survey evidence, but they suggest that earnings losses are less prevalent and less severe than previously thought.

The balance of this document proceeds as follows. The next section (Section 2) describes our data. Section 3 motivates and describes our methods. Section 4 presents our main results on the difference between military earnings when activated and civilian earnings when not activated. In Section 5, we summarize our findings and discuss why they might differ from DoD survey results. Section 5 also discusses how follow-on analyses will improve upon the estimates of earnings changes attributable to activation.

2. DATA

In this section we describe our data. We begin by describing the sample of reservists employed in this study. We then describe our data on civilian and military earnings and discuss our sample selection criteria. The section concludes with some descriptive statistics.

OUR SAMPLE

Our approach requires information on the civilian and military earnings of a sample of reservists. The sample for this analysis was created at the request of the Office of the Secretary of Defense—Reserve Affairs (OSD-RA) in 2003. The sample consists of 164,772 reservists activated in support of the Global War on Terrorism at some point during 2001 or 2002. For the purposes of selecting the sample, dates of activation were determined from the then current Defense Manpower Data Center (DMDC) GWT Contingency File.

For several reasons, this sample of reservists does not include all reservists activated since September 11, 2001. First, many reservists have been activated only since 2002. These reservists are not in our sample. Second, some reservists serving on active duty since September 11, 2001 are not included in the GWT Contingency File for administrative reasons.[7] Third, reservists serving on active duty for contingencies unrelated to the Global War on Terrorism are not included in the file. Fourth, OSD-RA and DMDC have worked to improve the completeness of the GWT Contingency File. After our sample was drawn using the then current GWT Contingency File, OSD-RA and DMDC identified several groups of reservists activated for the GWT through the end of 2002 who had been previously omitted from the GWT Contingency File.

Table 2.1 compares the characteristics of all reservists serving on active duty in the Army National Guard (ARNG), the Army Reserve (USAR), the Air National Guard (ANG), and the Air Force Reserve (AFR) in 2002 and 2003 as defined by the Reserve Pay File (see below) with the characteristics of Army and Air Force reservists in the sample of activated reservists employed in

---

[7] Reservists called to active duty under Title 32 following September 11, 2001 for purposes of airport security, guarding nuclear facilities, and other related homeland security activities were not legally considered activated in support of the Global War on Terrorism and so do not appear in the GWT Contingency File.

this report as defined by the 2003 version of the GWT contingency file. As can be seen, there is little difference across the GWT sample and the more comprehensive Reserve Pay File sample in terms of component or pay grade. However, there may be other differences between the two samples. Our follow-on analyses to this report will employ the more comprehensive Reserve Pay File sample.

Table 2.1 Proportion of Reservists by Year Serving on Active Duty, Sample, Component, and Pay Grade

	2002		2003	
	GWT	RPF	GWT	RPF
A. Component				
ARNG	44.9%	45.6%	45.2%	44.8%
USAR	25.6%	25.7%	26.6%	26.4%
ANG	17.1%	16.4%	16.2%	16.6%
AFR	12.4%	12.2%	11.9%	12.2%
B. Pay Grade				
E1-E4	36.4%	34.8%	30.4%	30.5%
E5-E9	51.9%	50.0%	57.8%	54.4%
O1-O3	4.9%	6.2%	4.4%	5.6%
O4-O6	6.8%	8.9%	7.3%	9.6%
n. obs.	109,159	470,684	106,267	421,257
Notes: Each cell represents the proportion of reservists in the column (by panel) with the characteristic indicated by the row label. The GWT sample refers to the sample of reservists used in this report. The RPF sample refers to all reservists serving on active duty in the year indicated. See below in this chapter for more details on sample definitions. *Data source*: RPF and WEX.				

CIVILIAN EARNINGS

Information on civilian earnings comes from SSA earnings records for calendar year 2001.[8] For each employee, employers file quarterly earnings information with SSA for the purposes of computing Federal Insurance Contribution Act (FICA) and Medicare taxes and Social Security and Medicare

---

[8]SSA subtracted from total Medicare taxable earnings recorded for the following Employer Identification Numbers: 529980000 (Coast Guard), 849980000 (Air Force – Reserve), 351819323 (Army – Reserve), 539990000 (Marine Corps – Reserve), 849990000 (Air Force – Active), 359990000 (Army – Active), 539990000 Marine Corps (Active), 349990000 (Navy – Active), and 349980000 [unknown]. Unlike FICA earnings, this earnings measure is not capped at a taxable limit.

benefits. Covered[9] employers are legally obligated to report earnings to SSA; deliberate reporting errors are criminal, and inadvertent errors are subject to penalties. As a result, SSA earnings data are believed to be of high quality and have been used in many empirical studies, including several studies related to the military.[10] The earnings measure provided to us by SSA for 2001, c_{2001}, does not include any military pay (neither inactive nor active duty reserve earnings).

MILITARY EARNINGS

We draw information on military earnings from the Reserve Pay File (RPF) maintained by the Defense Manpower Data Center (DMDC). The RPF records military pays and allowances received by reservists, as well as whether the pays qualify for the combat zone tax exclusion (CZTE). We use the RPF to compute the value of military compensation received in 2001, 2002, and 2003. This compensation includes basic pay, special pays (e.g., hostile fire pay (HFP)), basic allowances for housing and subsistence, and special allowances (e.g., the family separation allowance (FSA)). We also use information from the RPF to compute the value of the tax advantage that accrues to some pays and allowances (see below in this section for details).

The RPF distinguishes between reserve pay and active duty pay. Most frequently, reserve pay is earned for inactive duty training (IADT; e.g., one weekend per month). Active duty pay is earned for active duty training (ADT; e.g., two weeks during the summer) and for other time serving on active duty. In the equations below, we denote inactive duty reserve pay received in 2001 as r_{2001} and active-duty pay received by activated reservists in 2002 and 2003 as a_{2002} and a_{2003}.

The RPF has one significant limitation for the purposes of this analysis. The RPF only records active-duty pay for reservists serving in the Army Reserve, the Army National Guard, the Air Force Reserve, and Air National Guard. Navy and Marine Corps reservists receive active-duty pay through different compensation systems; as a result, their active-duty pays are not recorded in the RPF. Approximately 84 percent of all reservists serve in the

---

[9]Approximately 89 percent of U.S. workers work under covered employment (SSA, 2004).

[10] See, for example, Angrist, 1994, 1998 and Angrist and Krueger, 1994.

Army and Air Force.[11] Thus, while our analyses do not reflect the experience of reservists in all the Services, it will reflect the experience of the vast majority of the reserve force.

We adjust both civilian and military earnings for inflation using the CPI-U. All dollar amounts are expressed in $2003.

COMPUTING TIME ON ACTIVE DUTY

We combine information on rank and years of service with information from the RPF on basic pay received to compute time activated in a calendar year. For each calendar year from 2001 to 2003, we compute the fraction of time activated as the number of days of active-duty pay (given current rank and years of service) divided by 360 (30 days per month, 12 months per year).[12] We denote this measure of days activated in each year as: d_{2001}, d_{2002}, d_{2003}. In interpreting our results below, it is important to note that reservists participating in a standard two-week training exercise (Active Duty Training (ADT)) are paid from active-duty funds. Therefore, our count of active-duty days includes reservists serving during these standard two-week exercises. About 84 and 93 percent of our sample served on active duty for more than 15 days in 2002 and 2003, respectively.

ADVANTAGES OF USING ADMINISTRATIVE DATA

Using administrative data to study the impact of activation on earnings has several advantages over using survey-based data. One advantage is that these administrative data reduce measurement error in earnings. SSA civilian

---

[11]Authors' computation using the Reserve Component Common Personnel Data System.

[12]An alternative approach to dating activations is through DMDC's GWT Contingency File. That file is considered to be the best available evidence on activations and deployments for the Global War on Terrorism. Our SSA sample was defined using the GWT Contingency File.

Here, we use information on activation from the RPF because it includes all activations, whether or not they were due to the Global War on Terrorism. We expect earnings effects to depend primarily on total days activated, regardless of why a reservist was activated.

We also note that our analyses of the GWT Contingency File show that 9 percent of reservists have been deployed, but not activated. Discussions with DMDC suggest that this is partly explained by the fact that some reservists are not activated officially for the Global War on Terrorism even though they are deployed in support of a Global War on Terrorism contingency. The GWT Contingency File is therefore missing the begin and end dates of some activations that lead to deployment. We considered imputing activation dates as simply deployment dates. However, since activation must have occurred before deployment (typically, a month or more before), doing so would under-estimate the length of activation for these reservists.

earnings and military pay data from the RPF are both considered to be of very high quality. Other significant advantages of using administrative data for these purposes are that we can more precisely define which reservists are included in our analysis, what our earnings measure does and does not capture, and how our earnings measures relate to the period of activation (GAO, 2004).

These administrative data nonetheless have several limitations. First, we can only examine reservists in the Army Reserve, Army National Guard, Air Force Reserve, and Air National Guard. Second, our file only measures civilian earnings in 2001. As we explain further in the section below, this limitation causes us to focus on reservists who were activated for very short periods of time in 2001 and relatively long periods of time in 2002 or 2003. Having only one year of civilian earnings also imposes methodological limitations that we discuss in the concluding section to this report.

Finally, our data do not measure several potentially important sources of compensation while activated. Some civilian employers will pay the difference between military and civilian salaries for their reserve employees who are called to active duty. Reservists also accumulate points toward retirement when they serve on active duty. The expected present discounted value of these retirement points do not enter our computations. Activated reservists and their families are eligible for some other benefits (e.g., health care, access to the PX). These omissions cause us to underestimate military earnings received when serving on active duty. Our final report will address these shortcomings.

SAMPLE SELECTION AND DESCRIPTIVE STATISTICS

Our current analysis uses a subset of the original sample of 164,772 reservists drawn for OSD-RA. We drop the following records:

- 12,623 reservist who served in the Navy or Marine Corp Reserve, since the active-duty pay for these individuals does not appear in the RPF.
- 6,143 reservists who served in the Active Duty force (not merely on Active Duty as a reservist) during 2001. We drop these individuals because their pay as a member of the Active Duty force does not appear in RPF data or in our SSA data.

- 25,642 reservists who do not appear in the RPF.[13]
- 7,772 reservists whose Social Security Numbers SSA could not verify.
- Finally, for some analyses, we drop 17,123 reservists who have less than $10,000 of civilian earnings in 2001. This level of earnings is slightly below full-time employment at the federal minimum wage. ($10,712 = $5.15 per hour × 40 hours per week × 52 weeks.) We drop these reservists from some analyses because we are concerned that their reported earnings do not represent their true earnings potential. For example, some of these reservists might be students and some might be working in a sector that does not report earnings to SSA. Other reservists in our sample could simply be under-employed. Thus, the estimates from which we drop these individuals are an upper bound on true earnings losses.

Our primary sample is composed of 112,592 reservists; 95,469 reservists in our sample have 2001 civilian earnings of at least $10,000.

---

[13]Reservists might not appear in the RPF for a number of reasons. However, we could not determine with this particular sample exactly why, since the sample was drawn from data sources not available at RAND.

3. METHODS

We begin this section by describing our measure of earnings change. We then note that this measure, or concept of interest, is not the "counterfactual" concept. The counterfactual concept is arguably more appropriate, but we lack the data to estimate it at this time. Finally, we describe our methods and the statistics we compute using those methods.

THE CONCEPT OF INTEREST

Our concept of interest is the change in earnings of a reservist between a year in which the reservist was not activated at all (but did attend Inactive Duty Training (IDT)) and a year in which the reservist was activated for the entire year. If we observed a random sample of reservists who did not serve on active duty in 2001, but did serve on active duty for all of 2002 or 2003, we would estimate the change in earnings for each reservist as follows:

$$
\begin{aligned}
\Delta_{2001,2002} &= G\big[a_{2002}\big] - \big(c_{2001} + r_{2001}\big) \\
\Delta_{2001,2003} &= G\big[a_{2003}\big] - \big(c_{2001} + r_{2001}\big)
\end{aligned}
\tag{1}
$$

The second term on the right-hand side of Equation (1) is 2001 civilian plus inactive duty reserve earnings. In the balance of this document, we refer to this sum as 2001 civilian earnings.

The first term on the right-hand side of Equation (1) is more complicated. Civilian earnings are "gross earnings" (i.e., earnings before taxes). Therefore, an appropriate comparison to military earnings would also be "gross earnings" (i.e., before tax earnings). However, some components of military compensation—allowances and military pay received while serving in a combat zone—are not subject to federal taxation (neither federal income taxes, nor FICA and Medicare payroll taxes). Therefore, an appropriate comparison would be to the level of gross taxable earnings yielding the same net earnings as the military compensation package accounting for the tax advantage. The "G" function represents the required computations to adjust activated earnings for the federal tax advantage conferred on certain components of those earnings (i.e., it computes the taxable earnings required to yield the after-tax value of military compensation).[14]

This tax adjustment is conceptually similar to the tax advantage component of Regular Military Compensation (RMC). In practice, we compute the tax advantage assuming a reservist is not married, has no dependents, and no other income.[15] We will relax this simplifying assumption in our follow-on analyses. Unlike the conventional RMC calculation for the active forces, our tax computations consider FICA and Medicare taxes. We only consider the impact of federal taxes.[16] Some states also give preferential tax treatment to military pays and allowances. We do not account for these tax advantages in this analysis. Accounting for these state tax advantages would increase our estimates of earnings while activated.

We adjust 2002 and 2003 military earnings for the federal tax advantage. There is no need to adjust 2001 earnings, because the tax advantage for those not activated for more than a month is of trivial value. Those on IDT receive no allowances. Those on ADT receive allowances, but they are small. Neither group is likely to serve in a combat zone.

---

[14]The notation in Equation (1) and (2) is not strictly correct. Computing the value of the tax advantage requires not only knowledge of total military compensation, but also knowledge of the division of that total military compensation into its taxable and non-taxable components.

[15]We adopt this simplifying assumption because the data sources we use for the computations reported here do not include information on family structure (except as could be inferred from specific pays) or on civilian earnings of other family members. We note that this simplifying assumption has offsetting biases. The presence of a spouse and children would allow the reservist to use a different filing status with lower tax rates at each level of income and perhaps to claim the Earned Income Tax Credit (EITC). Offsetting this upward bias in taxes paid is the possibility that the activated reservist had in some year earnings not reported to SSA or that other members of the household (e.g., spouse or children) had earnings. Such earnings would imply higher taxes paid.

In follow-on work for this project, we will relax this assumption. We will impute family structure and the civilian earnings of spouses using other DoD survey data.

We note that the conventional Green Book figure for RMC for members of the Active Duty Force is also an approximation. It also assumes no other income. For members of the Active Duty Force, the assumption of no civilian earnings is plausible. The assumption of no non-labor earnings is perhaps also plausible. The assumption of no spousal earnings seems less plausible. That assumption will bias (downward) the value of the tax advantage of some components of military compensation.

[16]This includes accounting for the EITC and Social Security and Medicare taxes.

THIS IS NOT THE COUNTERFACTUAL CONCEPT

We note that this simple difference in earnings diverges in two important ways from the counter-factual question: How do earnings among activated reservists differ from what their earnings would have been in this period had they not been activated? The first divergence concerns the length of activation. Our lack of civilian earnings data for 2002 and 2003 implies that we can only reliably estimate total earnings in those years for individuals who can be presumed to have no civilian earnings (i.e., those activated for the entire calendar year).

Second, this difference compares military earnings in 2002 or 2003 to civilian earnings in 2001. However, if these reservists had not been activated, their civilian earnings in 2002 or 2003 would almost certainly have differed from their civilian earnings in 2001. We expect civilian earnings to rise with age. Over one or two years, workers gain experience, some acquire additional education and training, and most gain tenure with a specific employer, all of which would be expected to increase earnings.

In addition, around this expected path of earnings growth there is considerable variation. Workers vary in the fraction of the year they actually work and also in the number of hours they work and the amount of overtime they earn. Some workers have faster earnings growth; some have slower earnings growth. Thus, even in the absence of time on active duty, we would expect the earnings of some reservists to rise and those of others to fall. In some cases, we would expect those changes—even in the absence of significant time on active duty—to be large. With information on civilian earnings for 2002 and 2003, we could address this counterfactual question. We would identify a control group who was not activated or activated for relatively little time. We would then use their earnings growth over time as a proxy for expected earnings growth of those who were activated.[17] We will implement this methodological approach in analyses to be completed as part of follow-on analyses for the current project.

APPROXIMATING CHANGES IN EARNINGS

We cannot directly compute the differences in Equation (1) with our data, since we observe virtually no one in our sample who served on active duty for

___
[17] This approach is equivalent to the standard difference-of-differences estimator (Meyer, 1995).

all of 2002 or 2003 and did not serve on active duty at all during 2001.[18]
Instead, we approximate full-year civilian and full-year activated earnings by
extrapolating from observed partial-year earnings. The assumption here is
that civilian earnings per unactivated day of a reservist who was activated
for a small number of days in 2001 is equivalent to the civilian earnings per
unactivated day of a reservist who was not activated at all in 2001.
Similarly, we assume military earnings per activated day of a reservist who
was activated for almost all of 2002 or 2003 are equivalent to the military
earnings per activated day of a reservist who was activated for all of 2002 or
2003. We implement this approximation by generalizing Equation (1) as
follows:

$$
\Delta_{2001,2002} = G\left[\frac{360}{d_{2002}}a_{2002}\right] - \frac{360}{360-d_{2001}}\left(c_{2001}+r_{2001}\right)
$$

$$
\Delta_{2001,2003} = G\left[\frac{360}{d_{2003}}a_{2003}\right] - \frac{360}{360-d_{2001}}\left(c_{2001}+r_{2001}\right)
$$

(2)

The adjustments are a simple linear extrapolation of observed earnings based
on days of activation. For example, if a reservist was activated for 10
percent of 2001, we approximate full-year civilian earnings by inflating
observed civilian earnings by 10 percent. Conversely, if a reservist was
activated for 90 percent of 2002 or 2003, we approximate full-year activated
earnings by inflating observed military earnings by 10 percent (and then
applying the tax adjustment to the full-year value).[19]

It is important to note that these computations assume that there are no
civilian earnings in 2002/2003 for the period on active duty. Thus, our

---

[18]Note that to satisfy this requirement we would need to observe a reservist with
an initial activation of January 1, 2002 or January 1, 2003 and a deactivation date
later than December 31, 2002 or December 31, 2003.

[19] This simple approach to annualization implicitly assumes that the earnings
experience over days of active duty observed continue for the remainder of the year.
For example, if observed active duty pay includes 30 days of active duty pay received
in a combat zone out of a total of 60 days of active duty, our annualization method
assumes that, over a year, this reservist would serve half of his or her active duty
days in a combat zone.

computations do not account for any employer "top off,"[20] or for reservists receiving vacation pay while on active duty.

Below, we report estimates for all reservists and stratifying by time on active duty in 2001 and in 2002/2003. In our discussion, we pay particular attention to the estimates for reservists serving on active duty in 2002 and 2003 for relatively long periods (more than 270 days), but relatively short periods in 2001 (less than 91 days).[21] We do this for two reasons. First, our methods extrapolate from observed military earnings in a year to what earning would have been if the reservist had been on activate duty for the entire year. This extrapolation becomes more problematic as the fraction of the year actually served on active duty falls. Second, policymakers might be particularly concerned about the experience of reservists activated for a lengthy periods of time. Even moderate monthly losses over many months could easily accumulate to more than larger losses incurred over a small number of months.

Note also that we need some active-duty military compensation in 2002 or 2003 to extrapolate to the full year. Thus, we can only approximate earnings when activated for those who actually served on active duty in 2002 or 2003. For completeness, we report estimates for other patterns of activation (91 or more days in 2001; 270 or less days in 2002/2003) as well.

The resulting computations are roughly proportional to civilian earnings per month in 2001 and military earnings per month in 2003. However, we emphasize that the extrapolation to monthly earnings is not exact. Taxes are computed on an annual basis and the tax schedule is not linear. Thus, the pre-tax equivalent value of military earnings for one month on active duty is not simply one-twelfth the pre-tax value of military pay received for one year of active duty. The correct tax calculations would require knowing civilian earnings for 2002/2003, which we do not have in the data used for this analysis.

---

[20]By employer "top off," we mean the practice of some employers to pay reservists either their civilian pay or any difference between their civilian and military pay while activated.

[21]We consider total active duty days in a calendar year ignoring the possibility that days of active duty might not be served consecutively.

REPORTED STATISTICS

In Section 3, we report a number of statistics describing the change in earnings of reservists between 2001 and 2002 and between 2001 and 2003. First, we compute the mean change in earnings between 2001 and 2002 and 2001 and 2003. Second, we compute the fraction of reservists with earnings differences falling into the following ten absolute and percentage change categories: (1) greater than $20,000/greater than 40%; (2) $20,000 to $10,000/40% to 30%; (3) $10,000 to $5,000/30% to 20%; (4) $5,000 to $2,500/20% to 10%; (5) $2,500 to $0/10% to 0%; (6) -$2,500 to -$1/-10% to 1%; (7) -$5,000 to -$2,500/-20% to -10%; (8) -$10,000 to -$5,000/30% to 20%; (9) -$20,000 to -$10,000/-40% to -30%; and (10) less than -$20,000/less than -40%.

We compute these earnings change statistics overall and by days of activation and grouped rank: E1-E2, E3-E4, E5-E6, E7-E9, O1-O2, O3, O4, and O5-O6. We compute rank as of December 2001. When considering the results reported in Section 3, it is important to remember that reservists labeled E1-E2, for example, are likely to have been promoted to higher ranks in 2002 and 2003. This is true to a lesser extent of higher-rank reservists as well.

4. RESULTS

In this section, we present our results: estimates of the difference between civilian earnings when not activated for any part of 2001 and military earnings when activated for all of 2002 or 2003. We summarize these statistics in six tables, each of which has the same form. The first column in each table reports the number of observations contributing to the computations. The next three columns report annual civilian earnings in 2001 ($c_{2001} + r_{2001}$), annual military earnings in 2002 or 2003 (a_{2002}, a_{2003}), and the difference between these earnings figures (Δ_{2002}, Δ_{2003}), respectively. The next three columns report the percentage of reservists experiencing any earnings loss between years reservists did and did not serve on active duty, the percentage of reservists with earnings losses of $10,000 or more, and the percentage of reservists with earnings losses 10 percent or more, respectively. The final three columns report the percentage of reservists experiencing any earnings gain between years reservists did and did not serve on active duty, the percentage of reservists with earnings gains of $10,000 or more, and the percentage of reservists with earnings gains of 10 percent or more, respectively. Each table has two panels. Panel A reports results for the entire sample and Panel B reports results for the sample with 2001 civilian earnings of at least $10,000. An appendix contains tables that report a more complete description of the distribution of earnings changes derived from these data.

AGGREGATE RESULTS

We report results aggregated over 2002 and 2003 in Table 3.1 by days served on active duty in 2001, 2002, and 2003. The bottom row of the top panel presents results averaged over all reservists in our sample. Extrapolated annual average civilian earnings in 2001 for our sample is $40,300. Extrapolated average annual military earnings for this group in 2002 and 2003 is $50,400. Thus, earnings in this sample increase by an average of $10,200, or 25 percent, between 2001 and the year of active duty service. On a monthly basis, this amounts to a difference of $850. While mean earnings increase substantially on average in this sample, 28 percent of these reservists nonetheless experience some earnings loss. For 14 percent of all reservists in our sub-sample, the annual losses are $10,000 or more and for 20 percent of this group, these losses represent 10 percent or more of 2001 earnings. We conclude from Table 3.1 that most (72 percent) reservists serving on active duty during 2002 and 2003 experienced sizeable increases in total earnings, but an important minority experienced earnings losses of 10 percent or more.

The fourth row of Table 3.1 in Panel A presents results for reservists serving on active duty for less than 91 days in 2001 and more than 270 days in either 2002 or 2003. Extrapolated annual average civilian earnings for this group in 2001 are $39,300. Extrapolated average annual military earnings for this group in 2003 are $56,400. Thus, earnings in this sample increase by an average of $17,200, or 44 percent, between 2001 and the year of active duty service. On a monthly basis, this amounts to a difference of $1,433. While mean earnings increase substantially on average in this sample, 17 percent of these reservists nonetheless experience some earnings loss. For seven percent of this group, the annual losses are $10,000 or more and for 11 percent of this group, these losses represent 10 percent or more of 2001 earnings. Thus, Table 3.1 implies that reservists serving for longer periods of time on active duty in 2002 and 2003 were less likely to experience earnings losses than were reservists serving for relatively short periods of time in 2002 and 2003.

Table 3.1 2002/2003 Activated and 2001 Non-Activated Earnings ($000)
by Active-Duty Days

Active-Duty Days `01/`02-`03	N (,000)	`01 Civ. ($k)	`02/ `03 Mil. ($k)	Diff ($k)	Earnings Loss (%)			Earnings Gain (%)		
					Any	$10K+	10%+	Any	$10k+	10%+
A. Total sample										
0-90/0-90	54.1	39.6	44.9	5.3	38	19	29	62	37	54
0-90/91-180	19.8	40.3	50.7	10.4	24	12	16	76	54	68
0-90/181-270	23.5	40.0	53.7	13.7	20	10	13	80	60	72
0-90/271+	51.2	39.3	56.4	17.2	17	7	11	83	66	77
91+/0-90	14.2	37.6	42.0	4.4	37	23	30	63	43	58
91+/91-180	8.4	39.3	46.9	7.6	28	16	21	72	54	66
91+/181-270	13.3	43.4	50.4	7.0	32	19	23	68	51	61
91+/271+	28.0	43.8	52.3	8.5	29	17	21	71	56	64
All	212.5	40.3	50.4	10.2	28	14	20	72	52	65
B. 2001 earnings $10,000+										
0-90/0-90	47.2	44.4	46.9	2.4	44	22	33	56	29	47
0-90/91-180	17	46.0	53.7	7.6	28	13	19	72	47	62
0-90/181-270	20.4	45.2	56.2	11.1	23	11	15	77	54	68
0-90/271+	44.8	44.0	58.8	14.8	19	09	12	81	62	73
91+/0-90	10.6	48.8	47.3	-1.5	50	31	41	50	26	43
91+/91-180	6.6	48.1	50.9	2.8	35	21	27	65	43	56
91+/181-270	11	51.2	53.9	2.6	38	22	29	62	41	53
91+/271+	23.1	52.0	55.8	3.9	35	20	25	65	45	57
All	180.6	46.3	53.2	6.9	33	17	24	67	45	59

Notes: All figures in $2003. Sample size ("N") is simply the sum of the observations in 2002 and 2003. This number includes some double counting of individuals (i.e., people who were on extended active duty in 2002 and 2003). Data sources: SSA Master Earnings File/Reserve Pay File.

The other rows of Table 3.1 report the same computations for reservists with different patterns of active duty days in 2001 and 2003. Compared to reservists serving for long periods of time on active duty, average earnings gains are smaller and the fraction experiencing earnings losses is larger among reservists serving on active duty for 270 days or less. The average earnings gain across the other groups in Panel A of Table 3.1 is $8,370 and the percentage experiencing an earnings loss of 10 percent or more averages 31 percent.

The pattern of results in Panel A of Table 3.1 results from the fact that full-year equivalent military earnings rise with active-duty days. The increase in military earnings with days of active duty is largely attributable to the fact that the probability of receiving special pays, allowances, and

tax advantage (Table 3.2) increases with active-duty days because longer
activations are more likely to result in deployments that qualify for these
additional pays, allowances, and tax preferences. For example, 67 percent of
reservists serving more than 270 days in 2003 (but fewer than 91 days in 2001)
received the combat zone tax exclusion compared to 41 percent of reservists
serving 91-180 days in 2003 (but fewer than 91 days in 2001). A similar
difference exists in the fraction of reservists receiving hostile fire pay.
Table 3.3 shows how the various components of military earnings increase with
active-duty days. For example, the unconditional mean of the annualized value
of the tax advantage increases from $4,300 for reservists serving 0-90 active
duty days in 2003 to $9,900 for reservists serving more than 270 active duty
days in 2003.

Table 3.2 Percent Receiving Specific Military Pays and Allowances While Activated by Earnings Component and Active-Duty Days

Active-Duty Days `01/`02-`03	CZTE	HFP	FSA
A. 2002			
0-90/0-90	9	3	4
0-90/91-180	30	24	49
0-90/181-270	42	36	49
0-90/271+	40	31	51
91+/0-90	8	4	5
91+/91-180	23	19	20
91+/181-270	30	24	37
91+/271+	41	33	44
B. 2003			
0-90/0-90	20	8	17
0-90/91-180	41	36	58
0-90/181-270	51	47	62
0-90/271+	67	62	61
91+/0-90	18	5	8
91+/91-180	31	27	34
91+/181-270	50	48	44
91+/271+	63	57	43
Data source: Reserve Pay File.			

Table 3.3 Annualized Military Earnings While Activated ($000) by Earnings Component and Active-Duty Days

Active-Duty Days `01/`02-`03	Total	Pay		Allowances		Tax exclusion
		HFP	Other	FSA	Other	
A. 2002						
0-90/0-90	42.1	0.1	31.7	0.0	7.1	3.3
0-90/91-180	48.2	0.4	31.2	0.5	9.6	6.5
0-90/181-270	51.2	0.4	31.4	0.5	11.3	7.6
0-90/271+	55.6	0.3	34.6	0.5	12.4	7.8
91+/0-90	34.2	0.1	25.6	0.1	5.8	2.6
91+/91-180	46.4	0.3	29.5	0.2	10.6	5.8
91+/181-270	49.3	0.3	30.8	0.4	11.5	6.3
91+/271+	52.4	0.2	32.6	0.4	12.2	7.0
B. 2003						
0-90/0-90	52.0	0.2	38.5	0.5	8.6	4.3
0-90/91-180	53.6	0.6	33.9	1.2	10.3	7.5
0-90/181-270	55.2	0.9	33.7	1.7	10.3	8.6
0-90/271+	56.2	1.3	32.8	1.6	10.5	9.9
91+/0-90	46.4	0.1	34.8	0.2	7.5	3.7
91+/91-180	47.2	0.4	31.2	0.7	9.4	5.6
91+/181-270	51.6	0.8	32.5	1.0	10.1	7.2
91+/271+	52.7	1.1	31.8	1.0	10.5	8.3
Notes: All figures in $2003. Data source: Reserve Pay File.						

Panel B of Table 3.1 reports results for the sample of reservists with 2001 civilian earnings of at least $10,000. We make this restriction in Panel B to account for the fact that some reservists have very low civilian earnings because they are attending college, work in sectors of the U.S. economy not covered by Social Security (either legally or illegally), or are otherwise underemployed (i.e., not in stable employment). Policymakers might be most interested in understanding how activation impacts the earnings of reservists exhibiting some basic level of attachment to the traditional labor force (or, alternatively, for whom 2001 earnings are a good proxy for their civilian earnings potential, or, the earnings they forgo when activated).

As expected, average earnings gains in this more restricted sample are somewhat smaller and the fraction of reservists with earnings losses somewhat higher. Averaging across all reservists in the restricted sample, earnings increased by an average of $6,900. The fraction of reservists experiencing an income loss increases to 33 percent. Earnings increased by an average of $14,800 for reservists activated for fewer than 91 days in 2001 and more than

270 days in 2002 or 2003. The fraction of this group of reservists experiencing an income loss increases to 19 percent.

In as much as those with low civilian earnings are in school or have uncovered employment, the tabulations excluding them are probably more appropriate. However, some reservists are simply underemployed. For them, activation represents a real increase in earnings. In as much as the underemployed group dominates those with low civilian earnings, the tabulations in Panel A are more appropriate. Both groups are of substantive importance, so the concept of interest is probably somewhere between the tabulations in Panels A and B. In general, our discussion emphasizes the analyses of the entire sample. Thus, our results including the low income sample are biased in favor of finding larger gains and smaller losses.

2002 VERSUS 2003

Our results vary depending on whether we examine reservists serving on active duty in 2002 or in 2003. Panel A of Table 3.4 presents statistics on earnings changes between 2001 and 2003. Averaging over all reservists serving on active duty in 2003, we find earnings increase between 2001 and 2003 by an average of $13,800. About 23 percent of these reservists experience some earnings loss. For 12 percent of all reservists, the earnings losses are $10,000 or more and for 16 percent of this group, earnings losses represent 10 percent or more of 2001 earnings.

Table 3.4 2003 Activated and 2001 Non-Activated Earnings ($000) by Active-Duty Days

Active-Duty Days `01/`03	N (,000)	`01 Civ. ($k)	`03 Mil. ($k)	Diff ($k)	Earnings Loss (%)			Earnings Gain (%)		
					Any	$10K+	10%+	Any	$10K+	10%+
A. Total sample										
0-90/0-90	13.3	44.7	52.4	7.8	40	22	31	60	37	51
0-90/91-180	7.7	41.8	54.0	12.3	22	11	15	78	58	70
0-90/181-270	12.9	39.5	55.5	16.0	17	8	11	83	64	76
0-90/271+	40.0	37.2	56.5	19.4	13	5	8	87	71	81
91+/0-90	8.7	46.2	46.6	0.4	48	31	39	52	34	46
91+/91-180	3.9	41.3	47.5	6.2	31	18	24	69	52	62
91+/181-270	5.4	42.9	51.8	8.9	29	18	22	71	57	65
91+/271+	12.8	37.8	52.5	14.6	19	10	13	81	68	75
All	104.8	40.0	53.8	13.8	23	12	16	77	60	71
B. 2001 earnings $10,000+										
0-90/0-90	11.8	49.6	53.8	4.2	46	25	34	54	30	44
0-90/91-180	6.7	47.1	56.5	9.4	25	12	17	75	52	66
0-90/181-270	11.2	44.7	58.1	13.4	20	9	12	80	59	72
0-90/271+	34.6	42.0	59.1	17.1	15	6	9	85	67	78
91+/0-90	7.5	53.0	49.1	-3.9	56	36	46	44	23	37
91+/91-180	3.1	50.3	51.2	0.9	39	23	30	61	40	52
91+/181-270	4.3	51.9	56.0	4.1	36	22	28	64	47	57
91+/271+	9.7	48.3	57.8	9.5	25	13	17	75	57	67
All	88.9	46.1	56.7	10.5	27	14	19	73	53	65

Notes: All figures in $2003. Data sources: SSA Master Earnings File/Reserve Pay File.

Reservists serving on active duty in 2002 experienced smaller average earnings gains than did reservists serving on active duty in 2003 (Table 3.5). Again, averaging across all reservists serving on active duty in 2002, we find a mean earnings difference of $6,600, far less than the mean earnings change of $13,800 reported for reservists in 2003 (see Table 3.4). The fraction with earnings losses in 2002 is also considerably higher in 2002 than in 2003 (32 versus 23 percent [compare with Table 3.4]). Similar differences between reservists serving on active duty in 2002 versus 2003 are found in the sample that excludes low civilian earners (Panel B in Tables 3.4 and 3.5).

Alternatively, focusing on reservists with less than 91 days of active duty in 2001 and more than 270 days of active duty in 2003, we find earnings increase between 2001 and 2003 by an average of $19,400. About 13 percent of these reservists experience some earnings loss. For five percent of this group, the losses are $10,000 or more and for eight percent of this group, these losses represent 10 percent or more of 2001 earnings. For this group in

2002, we find a mean earnings difference of $9,200, far less than the mean earnings change of $19,400 reported for reservists serving more than 270 days of active duty in 2003. The fraction with earnings losses in 2002 is also considerably higher in 2002 than in 2003 (30 versus 13 percent). Similar differences between reservists serving on active duty in 2002 versus 2003 are found in the sample that excludes low civilian earners (Panel B in Tables 3.4 and 3.5).

Table 3.5 2002 Activated and 2001 Non-Activated Earnings ($000) by Active-Duty Days

Active-Duty Days `01/`02	N (,000)	'01 Civ. ($k)	'02 Mil. ($k)	Diff ($k)	Earnings Loss (%)			Earnings Gain (%)		
					Any	$10K+	10%+	Any	$10K+	10%+
A. Total sample										
0-90/0-90	40.8	37.9	42.4	4.5	37	18	28	63	37	54
0-90/91-180	12.1	39.4	48.6	9.2	25	12	17	75	51	66
0-90/181-270	10.6	40.7	51.5	10.9	24	12	16	76	55	67
0-90/271+	11.2	46.7	55.9	9.2	30	15	21	70	50	61
91+/0-90	5.5	23.9	34.6	10.7	20	10	15	80	57	76
91+/91-180	4.5	37.5	46.3	8.8	25	15	19	75	56	69
91+/181-270	7.9	43.7	49.4	5.7	34	19	24	66	47	58
91+/271+	15.2	48.9	52.2	3.3	37	22	28	63	45	55
All	107.7	40.5	47.1	6.6	32	16	23	68	45	60
B. 2001 earnings $10,000+										
0-90/0-90	35.4	42.7	44.6	1.8	43	21	32	57	29	48
0-90/91-180	10.3	45.3	51.8	6.4	30	14	20	70	44	60
0-90/181-270	9.2	45.7	53.8	8.2	27	13	18	73	48	63
0-90/271+	10.2	50.8	57.6	6.8	33	17	23	67	45	58
91+/0-90	3.1	38.6	42.8	4.2	36	18	28	64	33	57
91+/91-180	3.5	46.2	50.7	4.5	32	19	24	68	46	60
91+/181-270	6.7	50.7	52.5	1.7	40	22	29	60	37	50
91+/271+	13.4	54.6	54.4	-0.2	42	25	31	58	37	49
All	91.7	46.5	49.9	3.4	38	19	28	62	37	53
Notes: All figures in $2003. Data sources: SSA Master Earnings File/Reserve Pay File.										

The difference between the 2002 and 2003 results for the aggregate sample is largely attributable to relatively high military earnings received by activated reservists in 2003 compared to 2002. Reservists serving on active duty in 2002 had 2002 military earnings of $47,100 compared to $53,800 for reservists serving on active duty in 2003. The increase in military pay received while serving on active duty between 2002 and 2003 is due to a number of factors, including:

- The average pay grade of our sample of reservists increases between 2002 and 2003.

- The fraction of activated reservists receiving special pays and the combat zone tax exclusion increases across years (see Table 3.2). The incidence of special pays increases because reservists serving on active duty in 2003 are much more likely to be serving in a combat zone due to the inception of the Iraq War in that year.

- There were some structural changes to military pay including a small increase in basic pay and more substantial changes to hostile fire pay (from $150 to $225 per month) and the family separation allowance (from $100 to $250 per month) between 2002 and 2003.

In the sample of reservists serving on active duty for less than 91 days in 2001 and more than 270 days in 2002 or 2003, the difference in earnings changes across years appears to be largely attributable to differences in civilian earnings rather than military earnings. The group of such reservists serving on active duty in 2002 had 2001 civilian earnings of $46,700 compared to $37,200 for those reservists serving on active duty in 2003.

The most likely explanation for this difference in civilian earnings between these two groups is that the composition of who served on active duty changed between 2002 and 2003. Results stratified by rank (presented below) show smaller differences in civilian pay between 2002 and 2003.

Another difference between the two groups is Reserve component. The fraction of reservists in our sample serving on active duty in the Army Reserve and National Guard for more than 270 days increased from 55 to 89 percent between 2002 and 2003. It is possible that Air Force reservists have higher civilian earnings than Army reservists. These differences in composition (rank and component) could account for the difference in civilian earnings between the group of reservists serving for long periods of time in 2002 and those serving for long periods of time in 2003.

It is possible that the two groups differ in other ways as well. For example, reservists serving on active duty in 2002 may have had more specialized skills than those serving on active duty in 2003. It is also possible that the Reserve components call-up the most experienced reservists first and less-experienced reservists second. It is worth noting that the sample of reservists serving more than 270 days in 2002 is much smaller than the sample of reservists serving more than 270 days in 2003 (10,220 versus 34,588).

In follow-on work, we will explore the possibility that experience and specialization account for some of the differences we observe in civilian earnings across the two groups of activated reservists. We will explore this possibility using multivariate models to control simultaneously for component, rank, gender, age, region, and military occupation.

DISAGGREGATION BY RANK

In this section, we report earnings changes by rank. We report these more disaggregated results for two reasons. First, how activations impact the earnings of reservists of different rank is of independent interest to policymakers. If we found that some ranks are more likely to suffer losses or suffer larger losses, we might adopt policies to target additional compensation to them specifically.

Second, some of the variation in earnings changes we observed across years and across groups in the tables described in the previous section could be the result of heterogeneity in rank (i.e., some of the groups and years may include a higher proportion of Officers or higher-rank enlisted personnel). Ideally, our estimates of earnings changes would control for a wider set of characteristics (both observed and unobserved) than just rank and days of activation. As explained in the concluding section, follow-on analyses will employ a more comprehensive set of controls.

Panel A of Table 3.6 reports earnings changes between 2001 and 2002/2003 by grade for all reservists serving on active duty in our sample. The table shows that average earnings gains are greater for officers than for enlisted personnel and, within the enlisted force, average gains are larger junior enlisted reservists. Conversely, absolute and percentage losses are the smallest for the junior enlisted reservists. Otherwise, the distribution of percentage losses is fairly stable across rank.[22]

---

[22] There is little significant variation in active duty days across rank and year. The one exception is that E1-E2's are more likely to serve 91 or more active duty days in 2001. This makes sense since these individuals would have been attending basic training in that year.

Table 3.6 2002/2003 Activated and 2001 Non-Activated Earnings ($000) by Rank

Rank	N (,000)	'01 Civ. ($k)	`02/ '03 Mil. ($k)	Diff Δ ($k)	Earnings Loss (%)			Earnings Gain (%)		
					Any	$10K+	10%+	Any	$10K+	10%+
A. Total sample										
E1-E2	9.8	10.3	27.2	17.0	6	2	4	94	77	93
E3-E4	73.5	22.2	34.5	12.3	19	8	14	81	59	76
E5-E6	77.3	42.6	48.3	5.8	36	19	27	64	42	55
E7-E9	26.8	58.4	65.3	6.9	35	19	23	65	45	54
O1-O2	4.0	52.2	67.6	15.4	27	17	20	73	61	67
O3	7.0	65.8	88.3	22.5	22	14	15	78	69	71
O4	9.1	85.7	104.0	18.3	26	19	19	74	66	67
O5-O6	4.9	105.2	117.8	12.5	30	25	24	70	62	62
B. 2001 earnings $10,000+										
E1-E2	3.1	21.5	28.9	7.4	19	5	14	81	48	77
E3-E4	53.9	28.0	35.6	7.6	26	11	19	74	45	67
E5-E6	73.1	44.7	48.5	3.9	38	20	28	62	39	52
E7-E9	26.1	59.9	65.4	5.5	36	20	24	64	44	53
O1-O2	3.8	54.6	67.7	13.0	28	18	21	72	59	65
O3	6.8	67.6	88.4	20.8	22	15	16	78	68	70
O4	8.9	87.4	104.1	16.7	26	19	19	74	65	66
O5-O6	4.8	107.2	117.9	10.6	31	25	24	69	62	61

Notes: All figures in $2003. Rank is determined in December 2001. Sample size ("N") is simply the sum of the observations in 2002 and 2003. This number includes some double counting of individuals (i.e., people who were on extended active duty in 2002 and 2003). Data sources: SSA Master Earnings File/Reserve Pay File.

Panel B of Table 3.6 repeats the analysis, excluding the group of low-earners in 2001. Earnings losses increase most sharply as we move from Panels A to B among the two lowest-rank groups of enlisted reservists. These are exactly the group of reservists who we would expect to be either in school or underemployed in 2001.

Tables 3.7 and 3.8 report results by rank for reservists serving on active duty in 2003 and 2002, respectively. The basic patterns observed in Table 3.6 remain.

Table 3.7 2003 Activated and 2001 Non-Activated Earnings ($000) by Rank

Rank	N (,000)	'01 Civ. ($k)	'02 Mil. ($k)	Diff ($k)Δ	Earnings Loss (%)			Earnings Gain (%)		
					Any	$10K+	10%+	Any	$10K+	10%+
A. Total sample										
E1-E2	5.0	10.2	31.6	21.4	3	1	2	97	89	96
E3-E4	36.4	22.1	38.0	16.0	14	6	10	86	68	81
E5-E6	38.0	42.4	51.1	8.7	31	16	23	69	49	61
E7-E9	13.2	58.3	67.4	9.1	32	18	22	68	49	57
O1-O2	2.0	52.2	76.6	24.4	18	11	12	82	73	77
O3	3.5	65.7	96.0	30.3	16	11	11	84	76	77
O4	4.4	85.6	109.9	24.3	22	17	16	78	71	71
O5-O6	2.4	105.0	122.7	17.7	27	23	22	73	66	65
B. 2001 earnings $10,000+										
E1-E2	1.6	21.4	33.2	11.8	9	3	6	91	68	88
E3-E4	26.6	27.9	39.2	11.3	19	8	13	81	56	75
E5-E6	36.0	44.5	51.4	6.9	33	17	24	67	46	59
E7-E9	12.8	59.7	67.5	7.8	33	18	22	67	48	56
O1-O2	1.9	54.6	76.5	21.9	19	12	13	81	71	76
O3	3.4	67.4	96.1	28.7	17	11	12	83	75	77
O4	4.3	87.3	110.0	22.7	23	17	17	77	70	70
O5-O6	2.3	107.1	122.9	15.8	28	23	22	72	65	65

Notes: All figures in $2003. Rank is determined in December 2001. Data sources: SSA Master Earnings File/Reserve Pay File.

Table 3.8 2002 Activated and 2001 Non-Activated Earnings ($000) by Rank

Rank	N (,000)	'01 Civ. ($k)	'02 Mil. ($k)	Diff ($k)Δ	Earnings Loss (%)			Earnings Gain (%)		
					Any	$10K+	10%+	Any	$10K+	10%+
A. Total sample										
E1-E2	4.9	10.3	22.7	12.4	9	2	7	91	66	89
E3-E4	37.2	22.3	31.0	8.7	24	10	18	76	51	70
E5-E6	39.3	42.7	45.6	2.9	41	21	30	59	35	49
E7-E9	13.6	58.6	63.4	4.7	37	20	25	63	41	51
O1-O2	2.0	52.2	58.8	6.6	35	23	27	65	49	57
O3	3.6	66.0	80.9	14.9	27	18	19	73	62	65
O4	4.6	85.8	98.4	12.7	29	21	21	71	61	63
O5-O6	2.5	105.5	113.1	7.6	33	27	25	67	59	59
B. 2001 earnings $10,000+										
E1-E2	1.5	21.6	24.6	3.0	28	8	22	72	27	65
E3-E4	27.3	28.1	32.1	3.9	33	14	25	67	34	59
E5-E6	37.2	44.8	45.8	1.0	43	22	32	57	31	46
E7-E9	13.3	60.1	63.4	3.4	38	21	26	62	40	50
O1-O2	1.9	54.6	59.1	4.4	37	24	28	63	47	55
O3	3.5	67.8	80.8	13.1	27	18	19	73	60	64
O4	4.5	87.5	98.6	11.0	29	22	21	71	60	62
O5-O6	2.5	107.4	113.2	5.7	33	27	26	67	58	58

Notes: All figures in $2003. Rank is determined in December 2001. Data sources: SSA Master Earnings File/Reserve Pay File.

5. DISCUSSION

This document has reported on the results of early analyses of the effect of activation on the earnings of reservists. Our analysis here is limited to a sample of reservists activated for the Global War on Terrorism in 2001 or 2002. We measured civilian and military earnings for the Army and the Air Force reserve components using data from SSA (for civilian earnings in 2001) and DMDC (for military pay in 2001, 2002, and 2003). Annual civilian and military earnings were approximated based on days of active-duty service derived from the RPF. Our measure of military earnings accounts for the federal tax preference accorded allowances and earnings received while serving in a combat zone.

SUMMARY OF EARNINGS CHANGES

Averaging across all reservists in our sample, average earnings increased by $10,200 ($850 per month) between 2001 and the year in which these reservists served on active duty. About 28 percent of this sample had any earnings loss and about 14 percent had earnings losses of $10,000 or more. About 20 percent of this sample had earnings losses of 10 percent or more. Thus, in summary, most reservists in our sample experienced an earnings gain and that earnings gain was often large. However, a sizable fraction of reservists experienced earnings losses and those losses were sometimes also large.

Policy makers might be particularly concerned about reservists serving on active duty for extended periods of time. For these reservists, even small monthly earnings losses could accumulate to large annual losses. Furthermore, our methods rely on an extrapolation that is most appropriate for this group of reservists. For reservists serving on active duty for 90 days or less in 2001, average earnings increase by $17,200 ($1,433 per month) between 2001 and a year in which they served more than 270 days of active duty service. About 17 percent of this sample has any earnings loss and about six percent has earnings losses of $10,000 or more. About nine percent of this sample has earnings losses of 10 percent or more.

Earnings differences vary considerably by year and days of active duty service. Average earnings gains are smaller and the fraction with losses is larger in 2002 than in 2003. Furthermore, reservists who served 270 days of active duty or less in 2002 or 2003 also experienced smaller annual earnings gains and larger earnings losses than those serving more than 270 days. We note, however, that the extrapolation of earnings is more problematic for this group.

Much of the difference in estimated earnings changes across years and days of active-duty service can be attributed to differences in military earnings. The likelihood of receiving special pays and federal tax preferences increases with days of active-duty service in 2002 or 2003 and is, overall, considerably higher in 2003 than in 2002. Promotions and increases in various components of pay between 2002 and 2003 also contributed to the increase in the military earnings of activated reservists between 2002 and 2003.

Various interpretations of this increase in military pay are possible. First, we are comparing 2001 civilian earnings to 2002 and 2003 military earnings. We would expect civilian earnings also to rise over this interval. This study analyzes earnings changes. It does not analyze the counterfactual question: "What would earnings have been for an activated reservist had that reservist not been activated?" We will address this counterfactual question in follow-on analyses with new data from SSA on earnings of reservists who were not activated.

Second, some would argue that deployment specific pays, allowances, and tax preferences should not be included in a measure of earnings gains. Active duty forces also receive these deployment specific pays, allowances, and tax preferences. They are compensation for the additional inconvenience, effort, and danger of such deployments. In the language of labor economics, they could be viewed as "compensating wage differentials".

However, these pays, allowances, and tax preferences are cash to the reservist and his family. They are available to pay bills (e.g., a mortgage). They could be saved for future expenses. This document is not intended as an analysis of whether reservists are made better off by activation. As we discuss below, there are many other components of monetary, near-monetary, and non-monetary well being that we do not consider. Instead, we believe that it is most useful to view this analysis as focused on the narrow question of how earnings change when activated. For this purpose, these pays, allowances, and tax preferences should count as earnings.

Among reservists activated for less than 91 days in 2001 and more than 270 days in 2002 or 2003, the decrease in mean 2001 civilian earnings among those serving on active duty in 2002 and those serving on active duty in 2003 also played a role in determining differences in earnings changes. Much of this difference in civilian earnings is likely due to the increase in the fraction of our sample serving in the Army Reserve and Army National Guard between 2002 and 2003. It is also possible that other characteristics, especially those related to military specialty and experience, differ between those who served on active duty in 2002 and those who served on active duty in 2003.

These findings on earnings change attributable to activation are consistent with the findings of earlier research on military and civilian earnings. Analyses conducted for the 9th Quadrennial Review of Military Compensation indicate that Regular Military Compensation (RMC) for active duty soldiers is above the median for demographically similar civilians. RMC for reservists is computed from the same schedule as RMC for members of the active duty force (OSD-PR 2002). Furthermore, we might expect those reservists with the best civilian opportunities to work more hours at their civilian jobs, while those with relatively poor civilian labor market opportunities to work more hours in the Reserves. This later group would be expected to include many reservists who are "under-employed" or not working at all. Anecdotal evidence is consistent with this inference, as is the differences in results when we exclude reservists with low civilian earnings.

In addition, both basic pay and the value of some of the deployment specific components of compensation (e.g., FSA, HFP) have increased sharply in recent years. Furthermore, for many of our reservists, especially for those activated for most of the year, total compensation is well above RMC. Beyond RMC, reservists often receive FSA, HFP, and CZTE. As the tabulations in Table 3.2 show, the value of these forms of compensation can be substantial.

The results reported here are subject to several important caveats. First, these results are based on a pre-existing sample of reservists activated in 2001 and 2002 for the Global War on Terrorism. Second, our sample excludes reservists serving in the Navy and Marine Corps. Third, the approach taken here compares earnings prior to activation to earnings received when activated. Our analysis does not consider what would have happened to the earnings of reservists had they not been activated. Fourth, our estimates do not consider several sources of compensation received when serving on active duty. These include employer "top-off" and the expected present discounted value of accumulated retirement points.

Finally, these estimates refer to an important, but narrowly defined outcome: earnings. We ignore any increase in household costs, any business losses, any effects on spousal earnings, and any non-financial costs (or benefits) attributable to activation and deployment. Thus, standard compensation arguments imply that, inasmuch as the reserve components are experiencing recruiting and retention problems, the conventional incentive case for raising reserve compensation remains valid.

COMPARISON TO SURVEY-BASED ESTIMATES

The results reported here suggest that about one in four activated reservists has any loss and about one in five has an earnings loss of 10 percent or more. The results also indicate that earnings losses are less prevalent and severe among those reservists serving on active duty for extended periods of time. About one in six reservists serving on active duty for extended periods experiences any earnings loss and that less than one in ten experiences an earnings loss of 10 percent or more. This characterization of earnings changes attributable to activation is quite different from that suggested by stories reported in the popular press and by estimates of earnings changes generated from DoD survey data.

The difference between estimates reported here and those reported elsewhere is attributable to a variety of factors. Our data force us to focus on the effect of activations on Army and Air Force reservists activated in 2001 and 2002. Stories in the media and those derived from survey data apply to all reserve components and to reservists activated in other years.

Probably of greater importance, our results include the value of the tax advantage. DoD survey questions on this topic specifically request reservists to report earnings *before* taxes. They therefore do not incorporate the value of the tax advantage. Our estimates suggest that the tax advantage is a major component of earnings while activated, especially for reservists activated for long periods of time.

In addition, as with all survey research, there is ambiguity about how respondents understand survey questions on earnings loss (GAO, 2004). What earnings "losses" do respondents consider? What time frame do they use? How good is their recall of past earnings? Furthermore, the survey information on the timing and nature of the activation is limited. This limitation makes it difficult to stratify results by characteristics of the activation. Finally, survey response is never 100 percent complete, which can compromise the representativeness of the survey sample.

Compared to survey-based analyses, the analyses reported here, which rely on administrative data, allow us to be explicit about how earnings are defined (specifically, we include an approximation to the value of the tax advantage) and how our earnings measures relate to the period of activation. Missing data is not a major issue in our data, and our data contain high-quality measures of civilian and military earnings and dates of activation.

FOLLOW-ON ANALYSES

This document has reported early results of the impact of activation on the earnings of reservists based on the civilian and military earnings of a sample of activated reservists selected by DMDC and OSD-RA in 2003. These estimates are preliminary. Follow-on analyses as part of this project will employ more and better data on both civilian and military earnings. Specifically, we will

- *Expand the sample for which we have civilian earnings.* The analyses reported here are based on civilian earnings in 2001 for reservists identified as of mid-2003 as having been activated in 2001 or 2002 in support of the Global War on Terrorism. This restriction limits the extent to which we can generalize these results to the universe of reservists. SSA is currently preparing a new sample that will include civilian earnings for all reservists.

- *Append civilian earnings for 2002 and 2003.* The analyses reported here are limited by the availability of civilian earnings data for only 2001. This restriction limits our ability to control for year-to-year variation in earnings and normal earnings growth. It also forces us to emphasize earnings changes attributable to long activations. In the present study, we estimated annual civilian and military earnings using a simple linear extrapolation of measured earnings based on days of active-duty service. In our subsequent analysis, we will use a comprehensive and consistently defined measure of earnings from SSA that obviates the need to annualize earnings through extrapolation.

- *Include reserve pay data from the RPF for 2004.* Our current analyses only include military pay data through 2003. Clearly, more recent data would help inform the current policy debate.

These additional data will allow us to improve our methodological approach in a variety of ways:

- *Control for unobserved heterogeneity.* In the current paper, we compare activated and non-activated earnings. However, we do not know how these differences compare to the changes in earnings of reservists who have not been activated. In general, we expect civilian earnings of reservists (and especially of young reservists) to rise with age. In addition to how earnings change with activation, another policy-relevant question is how the change in earnings between, say, 2001 and 2002, for a reservist activated in 2002 differs from the change in earnings between those same years for a reservist who was not activated in 2002. Our new data set will contain the earnings of both activated and non-activated reservists, allowing us to implement standard difference-in-differences models of earnings changes, using unactivated reservists or those activated for only short periods as controls.

- *Account for overall variability of earnings.* In any sample of individuals, there are likely to be individuals whose earnings increase or decrease from year to year by some amount. Thus, we should not be surprised that some reservists in our sample see their earnings decline while some see their earnings increase. With data on both activated and non-activated reservists, we can estimate whether activations increase the extent to which we observe reservists with earnings losses in any given year.

- *Use regression modeling.* The current paper has used simple stratification to control implicitly for the effect of rank on earnings changes attributable to activation. Our final report will use regression modeling to control for multiple sources of observed population heterogeneity (e.g., component, age, rank, gender, military occupation). Regression modeling will also allow us to generate more precise estimates of the impact of partial years of activation on earnings and the impact of past activations on current earnings.

- *Apply an improved tax model.* The current paper assumes that every reservist is single and has no children. This assumption is clearly incorrect. We will impute family structure from DoD surveys and use that imputed information to compute better estimates of the federal tax advantage. Since we believe the federal tax advantage is a major reason why reserve earnings increase with activation, a better approximation of this tax advantage is potentially important. In practice, we suspect that the errors in our current method for computing the tax advantage are approximately offsetting. Reservists with spouses and children have larger deductions, which lower taxes, but these reservists are also more likely to have their total household earnings supplemented by spousal earnings, which could raise their marginal tax rates.

In addition to reporting more refined and disaggregated estimates of earnings changes attributable to activation, the final report will include an expanded discussion of the policy context and implications of these results for DoD policies related to reserve compensation. Finally, the final report will contain more discussion of the data sources employed in this study and some analysis of SOFRC data on earning changes.

SOME CONCLUDING THOUGHTS

These preliminary results suggest that earnings loss when activated for extended periods is less common than might be inferred from stories in the media and from DoD survey data. However, these results only consider the reservist's own earnings losses. Activation also sometimes involves increases in household costs, business losses, lower spousal earnings, and other non-financial costs (or benefits). Thus, standard compensation arguments imply that inasmuch as the reserve components are experiencing recruiting and retention problems, the conventional incentive case for raising reserve compensation remains valid.

In addition, we note that these results have some implications for proposals to "top off" earnings (i.e., pay the difference between military and civilian earnings for activated reservists) for federal employees or to provide tax credits to private employers who "top off" earnings for their employees. The earnings of reservists—in years when they are not activated and in years in which they are—are composed of many components. When establishing base (i.e., pre-activation) civilian compensation, it might be appropriate to include not only civilian earnings, but also regular reserve compensation (i.e., four drill periods a month and two weeks during the summer). Such an adjustment would likely increase the prevalence and severity of earnings loss. On the other hand, when considering military pay when on prolonged activation, it might be appropriate to consider not only basic pay, but also the other components of RMC (BAH, BAS, and their tax advantages) and deployment-specific pay (e.g., FSA, HFP) and the combat zone tax exclusion. This adjustment is likely to decrease the prevalence and severity of earnings loss. For long activations to combat zones, the effect of this second adjustment is likely to dominate, thereby lowering the projected cost of top-off proposals.

Prior to September 11, 2001, most reservists reasonably thought that the likelihood of being involuntarily activated for a lengthy period of time was low. Thus, even individuals who were at risk of suffering significant earnings losses when activated might nonetheless enlist or reenlist in the Reserves. However, it is likely that DoD's intensive use of the Reserves since September 11, 2001, has caused existing and potential reservists to revise their expectations upward regarding the likelihood of activation. Consequently, all else equal, we expect fewer individuals with large potential earnings losses to enlist or reenlist in the Reserves in the future, which suggests that the future aggregate level of earnings loss will be even smaller than we estimate here.

There are pros and cons associated with the departure from the Reserves of reservists with large potential earnings losses. On the one hand, perhaps reservists who stand to suffer large losses, like the self-employed or individuals who command large civilian salaries, are not a good match in aggregate for a Reserve force that DoD wishes to use with some frequency. On the other hand, many of these individuals could possess skills that are particularly valued by the Reserves, making their departure problematic for maintaining desired capabilities and readiness in the Reserves. How to compensate individuals with large earnings losses whom DoD wishes to retain is unclear and should be the focus of future research.

Regardless of what policies DoD enacts to address earnings loss in the future, we recommend that DoD consider providing reservists (and potential reservists) with more information about how their military earnings are likely to change when serving on active duty. Providing this information might help DoD avoid unwittingly recruiting and retaining reservists with the potential for large earnings losses and the attendant bad publicity that occurs because of this. Conversely, providing this information might also help the Reserves retain individuals who are unaware that their military earnings could increase significantly because of the special pays they receive and the tax preference accorded earnings received while serving in a combat zone.

BIBLIOGRAPHY

Angrist, Joshua D., "Lifetime Earnings and the Vietnam Era Draft Lottery: Evidence from Social Security Administrative Records," *American Economic Review*, June 1990, reprinted in *Labor Economics*, O. Ashenfelter (ed.), Edward Elgar Publishing Ltd., 1994.

Angrist, Joshua D., and Alan Krueger, "Why Do World War II Veterans Earn More Than Nonveterans?," *Journal of Labor Economics*, January 1994.

Asch, Beth J., and James R. Hosek. 1999. Military Compensation: Trends and Policy Options. Santa Monica, CA: RAND DB-273-OSD.

Asch, Beth J., James R. Hosek, and John T. Warner. 2001. An Analysis of Pay for Enlisted Personnel. Santa Monica, CA: RAND DB-344-OSD.Angrist, Joshua D., "Estimating the Labor Market Impact of Voluntary Military Service Using Social Security Data on Military Applicants," *Econometrica*, March 1998.

Defense Manpower Data Center (DMDC), "May 2004 Status of Forces Survey of Reserve Component Members: Distraction, Datasets, and Codebook," Arlington, VA: Survey and Program Evaluation Division, DMDC, 2005

Hosek, James R., and Jennifer Sharp. 2001. Keeping Military Pay Competitive: The Outlook for Civilian Wage Growth and Its Consequences. Santa Monica, CA: RAND IP-205-A.

Hosek, James R., Christine E. Peterson, Jeannette Van Winkle, and Hui Wang. 1992. A Civilian Wage Index for Defense Manpower. Santa Monica, CA: RAND R-4190-FMP.

Meyer, Bruce. "Natural and Quasi-Experiments in Economics." *Journal of Business and Economic Statistics*. 13:2 (April 1995), 151-161.

Office of the Under Secretary of Defense for Personnel and Readiness (OSD-PR). 2002. Report of the Ninth Quadrennial Review of Military Compensation, Volume 1. Washington, DC: Department of Defense, OSD-PR.

Social Security Administration (SSA), "Annual Statistical Supplement," Washington: Office of Policy, SSA, 2004.

U.S. General Accounting Office (GAO), "Military Pay: Army National Guard Personnel Mobilized to Active Duty Experienced Significant Pay Problems," Report to the Chairman, Subcommittee on National Security, Emerging Threats, and International Relations, Committee on Government Reform, House of Representatives, GAO-04-89, November 2003.

U.S. General Accounting Office (GAO), "Military Personnel: DOD Needs More Data Before It Can Determine If Costly Changes to the Reserve Retirement System Are Warranted," Report to Congressional Committees, GAO-04-1005, September 2004.

APPENDIX TABLES

Table A.1 Distribution of the Difference Between 2001 Civilian Earnings and 2003 Military Earnings by Days of Active-Duty Service

Active-Duty Days '01/'03	N (,000)	Losses					Gains				
		>20	10-19.9	5-9.9	2.5-4.9	0-2.4	0-2.4	2.5-4.9	5-9.9	10-19	20<
A. Total sample											
0-90/0-90	13.3	12	10	8	5	5	6	6	11	19	18
0-90/91-180	7.7	5	5	5	3	4	4	5	11	25	34
0-90/181-270	12.9	4	4	4	2	3	4	4	11	23	41
0-90/271+	40.0	2	3	3	2	2	3	4	9	23	48
91+/0-90	8.7	18	13	8	4	5	4	5	9	18	16
91+/91-180	3.9	11	8	6	3	4	4	4	8	22	29
91+/181-270	5.4	10	7	5	3	3	3	3	7	20	37
91+/271+	12.8	6	4	4	2	3	3	3	7	20	48
All	104.8	6	6	5	3	3	4	4	9	22	38
B. 2001 earnings $10,000+											
0-90/0-90	11.8	14	11	9	5	6	6	6	12	16	13
0-90/91-180	6.7	6	6	5	3	4	5	5	13	25	27
0-90/181-270	11.2	5	4	4	3	4	4	5	12	25	34
0-90/271+	34.6	3	3	3	2	3	3	4	10	26	41
91+/0-90	7.5	21	15	9	5	5	5	6	11	14	10
91+/91-180	3.1	13	10	8	4	5	5	5	10	22	18
91+/181-270	4.3	13	9	7	4	3	4	4	09	21	26
91+/271+	9.7	8	6	5	3	3	4	4	10	23	34
All	88.9	8	6	5	3	4	4	5	11	23	31
Data sources: SSA Master Earnings File/Reserve Pay File.											

Table A.2 Distribution of the Percentage Difference Between 2001 Civilian Earnings and 2003 Military Earnings by Days of Active-Duty Service

Active-Duty Days `01/`03	N (,000)	Change in Earnings `01-`03 (%)									
		Losses					Gains				
		>40	30-39	20-29	10-19	0-9	0-9	10-19	20-29	30-39	40<
A. Total sample											
0-90/0-90	13.3	7	6	8	9	10	9	7	6	4	33
0-90/91-180	7.7	2	3	4	6	7	8	8	7	7	49
0-90/181-270	12.9	2	2	3	4	6	7	7	7	6	55
0-90/271+	40.0	1	1	2	4	5	6	7	7	6	61
91+/0-90	8.7	12	8	10	10	9	7	6	4	3	33
91+/91-180	3.9	6	5	6	7	7	7	6	5	4	47
91+/181-270	5.4	5	4	6	7	7	6	5	5	4	51
91+/271+	12.8	2	2	4	5	6	6	5	5	4	61
All	104.8	3	3	4	6	7	7	6	6	5	53
B. 2001 earnings $10,000+											
0-90/0-90	11.8	8	7	9	10	11	10	8	6	5	25
0-90/91-180	6.7	3	3	5	7	8	9	9	8	8	41
0-90/181-270	11.2	2	2	3	5	7	9	9	8	7	48
0-90/271+	34.6	1	1	3	4	6	7	8	8	8	55
91+/0-90	7.5	14	9	11	11	10	8	7	5	4	21
91+/91-180	3.1	7	6	7	9	9	9	7	6	5	34
91+/181-270	4.3	6	5	8	9	8	8	7	6	5	39
91+/271+	9.7	3	3	5	7	8	7	7	6	6	49
All	88.9	4	3	5	7	8	8	8	7	6	44
Data sources: SSA Master Earnings File/Reserve Pay File.											

Table A.3 Distribution of the Difference Between 2001 Civilian Earnings and 2002 Military Earnings by Days of Active-Duty Service

Active-Duty Days `01/`02	N (,000)	Change in Earnings `01-`02 (%)									
		Losses					Gains				
		>20	10-19.9	5-9.9	2.5-4.9	0-2.4	0-2.4	2.5-4.9	5-9.9	10-19.9	20<
A. Total sample											
0-90/0-90	40.8	8	10	8	5	5	6	6	13	22	15
0-90/91-180	12.1	6	6	5	4	5	5	6	13	25	26
0-90/181-270	10.6	6	6	5	3	4	5	5	12	24	30
0-90/271+	11.2	8	8	6	4	4	5	5	11	21	28
91+/0-90	5.5	5	4	4	3	3	4	5	15	39	18
91+/91-180	4.5	9	6	5	3	3	4	4	11	27	29
91+/181-270	7.9	10	9	7	4	4	4	5	10	21	26
91+/271+	15.2	13	9	7	4	4	5	5	9	19	26
All	107.7	8	8	7	4	5	5	6	12	23	22
B. 2001 earnings $10,000+											
0-90/0-90	35.4	10	11	10	6	6	7	7	14	17	11
0-90/91-180	10.3	7	7	6	5	5	6	7	14	24	20
0-90/181-270	9.2	6	7	6	4	4	5	6	13	25	23
0-90/271+	10.2	8	8	7	4	4	5	6	12	22	23
91+/0-90	3.1	10	8	7	5	6	7	9	17	17	15
91+/91-180	3.5	11	7	6	4	4	5	5	12	25	21
91+/181-270	6.7	12	11	8	5	5	5	6	11	20	17
91+/271+	13.4	15	10	7	5	5	5	5	11	19	18
All	91.7	10	9	8	5	5	6	6	13	20	17
Data sources: SSA Master Earnings File/Reserve Pay File.											

Table A.4 Distribution of the Percentage Difference Between 2001 Civilian Earnings and 2002 Military Earnings by Days of Active-Duty Service

Active-Duty Days `01/`02	N (,000)	Change in Earnings `01-`02 (%)									
		Losses					Gains				
		>40	30-39	20-29	10-19	0-9	0-9	10-19	20-29	30-39	40<
A. Total sample											
0-90/0-90	40.8	6	6	8	9	9	9	8	6	5	36
0-90/91-180	12.1	3	3	5	6	8	9	8	7	6	45
0-90/181-270	10.6	2	3	5	6	8	9	8	7	6	46
0-90/271+	11.2	3	4	6	8	9	9	9	7	6	40
91+/0-90	5.5	4	3	4	4	4	4	4	4	3	65
91+/91-180	4.5	4	3	5	6	6	6	6	5	5	53
91+/181-270	7.9	5	5	7	9	10	8	6	5	4	42
91+/271+	15.2	6	6	7	9	9	8	7	6	5	38
All	107.7	5	5	6	8	9	8	7	6	5	41
B. 2001 earnings $10,000+											
0-90/0-90	35.4	7	6	9	10	10	10	9	7	6	26
0-90/91-180	10.3	3	4	6	8	10	10	9	8	7	35
0-90/181-270	9.2	3	3	5	7	9	10	9	8	7	39
0-90/271+	10.2	3	4	6	9	10	10	9	8	7	34
91+/0-90	3.1	8	5	7	8	8	7	7	7	6	38
91+/91-180	3.5	6	4	7	7	8	8	7	7	6	40
91+/181-270	6.7	6	6	8	10	11	10	8	6	5	31
91+/271+	13.4	7	6	8	10	10	9	7	6	5	30
All	91.7	5	5	8	9	10	10	9	7	6	31

Data sources: SSA Master Earnings File/Reserve Pay File.

Table A.5 Distribution of the Difference Between 2001 Civilian Earnings and 2003 Military Earnings by Rank

| | N | Change in Earnings `01-`03 (%) | | | | | | | | | |
| | | Losses | | | | | Gains | | | | |
Rank	(,000)	>20	10-19.9	5-9.9	2.5-4.9	0-2.4	0-2.4	2.5-4.9	5-9.9	10-19.9	20<
A. Total sample											
E1-E2	5.0	0	1	1	1	1	1	1	6	30	59
E3-E4	36.4	2	3	3	2	3	3	4	10	28	40
E5-E6	38.0	9	8	6	4	4	5	5	10	20	29
E7-E9	13.2	10	8	7	4	4	4	5	9	17	33
O1-O2	2.0	7	4	3	2	2	2	2	5	14	59
O3	3.5	7	4	2	1	2	2	2	4	11	65
O4	4.4	13	4	3	1	1	2	2	4	9	62
O5-O6	2.4	18	5	2	1	1	1	2	3	8	59
B. 2001 earnings $10,000+											
E1-E2	1.6	1	2	2	2	2	3	4	16	39	29
E3-E4	26.6	3	5	5	3	4	5	6	14	31	25
E5-E6	36.0	9	8	7	4	5	5	5	11	22	25
E7-E9	12.8	10	8	7	4	4	5	5	10	17	31
O1-O2	1.9	8	4	3	2	2	2	2	5	14	57
O3	3.4	8	4	2	1	2	2	2	4	11	64
O4	4.3	13	4	3	1	2	2	2	4	9	61
O5-O6	2.3	19	5	2	1	1	1	2	4	8	58

Notes: Rank is determined in December 2001. Data sources: SSA Master Earnings File/Reserve Pay File.

Table A.6 Distribution of the Percentage Difference Between 2001 Civilian Earnings and 2003 Military Earnings by Rank

Rank	N (,000)	Change in Earnings `01-`03 (%)									
		Losses					Gains				
		>40	30-39	20-29	10-19	0-9	0-9	10-19	20-29	30-39	40<
A. Total sample											
E1-E2	5.0	0	0	1	1	1	1	1	1	1	92
E3-E4	36.4	2	2	3	3	4	5	5	5	5	67
E5-E6	38.0	5	4	6	8	8	8	8	7	6	40
E7-E9	13.2	3	4	6	9	11	11	9	8	7	33
O1-O2	2.0	2	2	4	4	6	5	6	7	6	58
O3	3.5	2	2	3	4	5	6	6	7	6	58
O4	4.4	4	3	4	5	6	7	7	7	7	50
O5-O6	2.4	7	3	5	6	6	7	7	6	7	46
B. 2001 earnings $10,000+											
E1-E2	1.6	1	1	2	2	3	3	4	4	5	75
E3-E4	26.6	3	3	4	5	6	6	6	6	6	55
E5-E6	36.0	5	4	6	8	9	9	8	7	6	37
E7-E9	12.8	3	4	6	9	11	11	9	8	7	31
O1-O2	1.9	2	2	4	4	6	5	6	7	6	56
O3	3.4	2	2	3	4	5	6	6	7	6	57
O4	4.3	4	3	4	5	6	7	7	7	7	49
O5-O6	2.3	7	4	5	6	6	8	7	6	7	45

Notes: Rank is determined in December 2001. Data sources: SSA Master Earnings File/Reserve Pay File.

Table A.7 Distribution of the Difference Between 2001 Civilian Earnings and 2002 Military Earnings by Rank

Rank	N (,000)	Change in Earnings `01-`02 (%)									
		Losses					Gains				
		>20	10-19.9	5-9.9	2.5-4.9	0-2.4	0-2.4	2.5-4.9	5-9.9	10-19.9	20<
A. Total Sample											
E1-E2	4.9	1	2	2	2	2	3	5	18	48	18
E3-E4	37.2	4	6	6	4	5	5	6	14	30	20
E5-E6	39.3	10	11	9	6	6	6	6	12	18	17
E7-E9	13.6	11	10	7	5	5	5	5	11	19	22
O1-O2	2.0	14	9	5	3	4	4	3	9	16	33
O3	3.6	12	6	4	2	2	3	3	6	15	47
O4	4.6	16	5	3	2	2	2	2	5	12	49
O5-O6	2.5	22	5	3	1	2	2	2	5	9	49
B. 2001 earnings $10,000+											
E1-E2	1.5	2	5	8	5	7	10	13	22	21	6
E3-E4	27.3	5	8	8	5	6	7	8	18	26	8
E5-E6	37.2	11	11	9	6	6	7	6	12	18	13
E7-E9	13.3	11	10	8	5	5	5	6	12	19	20
O1-O2	1.9	15	10	5	3	5	4	3	9	17	30
O3	3.5	12	6	4	3	2	3	3	6	15	45
O4	4.5	16	5	3	2	2	2	2	6	12	48
O5-O6	2.5	22	5	3	1	2	2	2	5	10	48

Notes: Rank is determined in December 2001. Data sources: SSA Master Earnings File/Reserve Pay File.

Table A.8 Distribution of the Percentage Difference Between 2001 Civilian Earnings and 2002 Military Earnings by Rank

Rank	N (,000)	Change in Earnings `01-`02 (%)									
		Losses					Gains				
		>40	30-39	20-29	10-19	0-9	0-9	10-19	20-29	30-39	40<
A. Total sample											
E1-E2	4.9	2	1	2	2	2	2	2	2	2	82
E3-E4	37.2	4	4	5	6	6	6	5	5	4	55
E5-E6	39.3	6	6	8	10	11	10	8	6	5	29
E7-E9	13.6	3	4	7	10	12	12	11	9	7	25
O1-O2	2.0	7	5	7	7	8	8	7	7	4	39
O3	3.6	4	4	5	7	8	8	8	8	7	43
O4	4.6	5	4	5	7	8	8	9	8	7	39
O5-O6	2.5	8	5	6	8	7	9	8	8	7	36
B. 2001 earnings $10,000+											
E1-E2	1.5	5	4	6	7	6	6	7	6	7	45
E3-E4	27.3	5	5	7	8	8	8	7	7	6	39
E5-E6	37.2	6	6	9	11	11	11	8	7	6	25
E7-E9	13.3	3	5	7	11	13	12	11	9	7	23
O1-O2	1.9	8	6	7	8	9	8	7	7	4	36
O3	3.5	4	4	5	7	8	8	8	8	7	41
O4	4.5	5	4	5	7	8	8	9	8	7	38
O5-O6	2.5	8	5	6	8	7	9	8	8	7	35

Notes: Rank is determined in December 2001. Data sources: SSA Master Earnings File/Reserve Pay File.